THE AMERICAN SAILING ASSOCIATION'S
LET'S GO WINDSURFING

THE AMERICAN SAILING ASSOCIATION'S
LET'S GO
WINDSURFING

Algis Steponaitis

Illustrations by Ron Carboni

HEARST MARINE BOOKS

New York

Library of Congress Cataloging-in-Publication Data
Steponaitis, Algis.
    The American Sailing Association's let's go windsurfing / Algis
Steponaitis ; illustrations by Ron Carboni.
        p.   cm.
    Includes index.
    ISBN 0-688-13477-7
    1. Windsurfing—United States.   I. American Sailing Association.
II. Title.   III. Title: Let's go windsurfing.
GV811.63.W56S74   1994
797.3'3—dc20   94-6818
                                                            CIP

Printed in the United States of America

First Edition

1   2   3   4   5   6   7   8   9   10

BOOK DESIGN BY MICHAEL MENDELSOHN MM DESIGN 2000, INC.

Foreword

A Successful Recipe for Windsurfing

THE INGREDIENTS

Lots of water
1 surfboard
1 sail
1 certified school of instruction
10 parts fun

THE INSTRUCTIONS

Take the above ingredients, mix them together, and what you get is windsurfing. It could be the most exciting and gratifying sport you will ever learn.

When I began windsurfing fifteen years ago, there were ingredients missing from the above recipe. There was limited instructional information and only primitive equipment. Over the years, the recipe has been improved. Dry-land techniques, simulators, certified schools of instruction, equipment, and instructional manuals are just a few of the extra ingredients that have made windsurfing easier.

Algis Steponaitis and I have been perfecting the windsurfing recipe for many years now. Algis has devoted his life to windsurfing education by developing a nationwide program to certify windsurfing instructors.

Jeff "Coach" Hughes has been a windsurfing instructor since 1978 and is a WIA Instructor Trainer. He is the owner and school director of Big Winds and Front Street Sailboard in Hood River, Oregon, one of the top windsurfing retail, school, and rental operations in the country.

The six-level lesson system that Windsurfing Instructors of America (WIA) offers to instructors, students, and schools has made windsurfing more fun than ever.

Add your own ingredients to our recipe and—let's get cooking.

Jeff "Coach" Hughes

Acknowledgments

I would like to thank the American Sailing Association for its support, and especially Harry Munns for getting this book project started.

Thanks also to Windsurfing Instructors of America trainers Richard Ferrari of Spinnaker Sailing, Mountain View, California, Jeff "Coach" Hughes of Big Winds, Hood River, Oregon, and Jeff Craft of SF School of Windsurfing, San Francisco, California, for their support. My wife, Petra, has helped with the illustrations and given me valuable input throughout the writing of this book.

You and the American Sailing Association

It only takes a few minutes to get the boat or sailboard ready. It's a beautiful, sunny day, and a warm breeze rustles the leaves and fluffs your hair. Then, with a little push from the dock or shore, you're off skimming across the water's surface on your way to new adventure.

That's what sailing is all about. You will join thousands of other people who fall under the spell of the sailing dream each year. Your new life will include the thrill of exploring new coves and harbors, racing against your friends, or just sliding over the water pushed by the wind's gentle hands.

The American Sailing Association's Small Boats and Boards program was established to make your sailing experiences safer and more

fun. Certification means you get an organized curriculum taught by a professional instructor. Certified sailors enjoy a higher level of ability, greater enjoyment, and more confidence.

In 1983, the ASA brought uniform standards to sailing education. Since then, thousands of people have been certified to ASA standards at both the student and instructor levels. Most of these people are no different from you. They have learned everything from windsurfing in their own backyards to crossing the world's oceans using only the stars, moon, and planets to guide their way.

We hope you will continue to grow as a sailor and include ASA certification in your sailing education. You may want to race, cruise, teach, or even go to the Olympics or the America's Cup. Your desire and imagination are your only limits.

Contact ASA headquarters for complete information on certification, educational products, services, and membership: American Sailing Association, 13922 Marquesas Way, Marina del Rey, CA 90292; telephone (310) 822-7171, fax (310) 822-4741.

America's Sail Education Authority

Contents

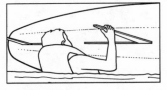

THE AMERICAN SAILING ASSOCIATION'S
LET'S GO WINDSURFING

Introduction

Windsurfing is a water sport that originated in the United States in the late 1960s and became an Olympic sport in 1984. If you enjoy water, wind, and being outdoors, you will love windsurfing.

Windsurfing is a family sport. Today, millions of men, women, and children from the ages of six to eighty-six participate worldwide in this exhilarating activity.

I have been windsurfing since 1974, and every time I go out I feel great. This sport has kept me healthy and has always given me a sense of well-being. Furthermore, there is always the challenge of improving one's own windsurfing skills.

As with any other sport, there are various skill levels. Windsurfing has six recreational levels. You can also specialize in other aspects of windsurfing such as *racing, speed, wave, touring, and freestyle windsurfing*.

The only thing hindering anyone from participating in this exciting sport are serious health problems, not being able to swim, or not being able to dive out from underneath a windsurfing board.

As a complement to this book, you can sign up for a Level-one windsurfing course at your local American Sailing Association (ASA) or Windsurfing Instructors of America (WIA) certified windsurfing school.

Only a certified instructor can best answer your questions, provide proper equipment, and help you to correct errors immediately.

In *Let's Go Windsurfing*, I'll cover recreational windsurfing, which will introduce you to the sport and give you the knowledge needed to windsurf in light wind conditions. Let's go windsurfing.

CHAPTER I
The Basics

Beginning to Windsurf

The first thing to learn about and get familiar with are the parts of the windsurfing board, how to determine wind direction, the appropriate places to go windsurfing, and what to wear.

Today, there are a wide variety of shapes and designs in boards and rigs. There is constant change and innovation in the windsurfing industry. The best way for a consumer to keep up with these changes is through windsurfing magazines. The type of materials used in the manufacture of windsurfing boards will have an effect on the cost of the product and its weight. You can also receive information through your local dealer on new windsurfing products and what materials are used in the manufacture of windsurfing boards.

Windsurfing boards can be placed into three specific groups: long boards that displace water; short boards for planing; and a combination of the previous two, the transition or giant slalom board.

Displacement boards displace water and have a lot of volume, over two hundred twenty liters. They are between eleven and a half and twelve and a half feet long, and perform very well in light to moderate wind conditions.

Planing boards ride on top of the water, are used in high winds, and have a volume of one hundred fifty liters or less. They come in lengths of nine feet or shorter. If the wind does drop below planing conditions, the short board also will displace water, but will perform poorly in light wind conditions.

Windsurfing boards that have both planing and displacement qualities are a compromise and will perform average in light or high wind

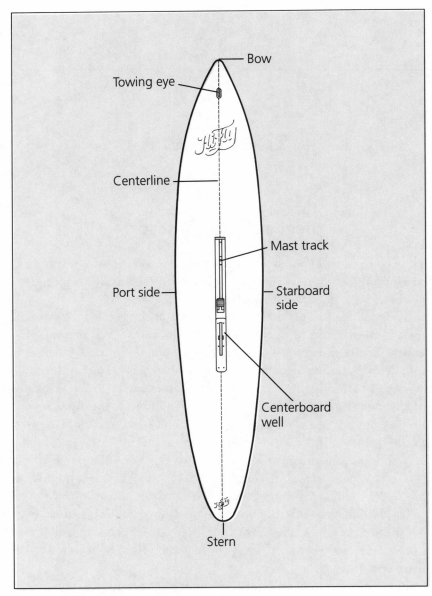

Recreational Windsurfing Board

conditions. The transition board will have a volume of one hundred fifty to two hundred twenty liters, and have a length between ten feet and eleven and a half feet.

PARTS OF A RECREATIONAL WINDSURFING BOARD

Bow: Front of the board

Centerboard: Stabilizes the board and reduces the tendency of the board to drift sideways

Centerboard Well: The opening where the centerboard is inserted

Fin: Gives the board directional stability and assists the centerboard to avoid drifting sideways

Mast Track: Where the rig is attached to the board

Port: The left side when looking toward the front

Recreational Board: Stable board with a length ranging from eleven feet to twelve feet, six inches and displacing a volume of two hundred twenty or more liters

Starboard: The right side when looking toward the front

Stern: Back of the board

Towing Eye: Near the bow of the board; used for towing or securing the windsurfing board to a dock or boat with a line

---

The recreational long board should be your choice when beginning to windsurf. You will be able to use and enjoy this type of board in most sailing areas across the country.

Windsurfing terminology is important for you to understand, as well as how the various parts function. Here is some basic terminology to begin with.

The Rig

The rig refers to all the parts on a windsurfing board that are above the board's surface. These parts include the sail and everything attached to it.

Rigging is the assembling of all the parts of the rig. The rig is essentially the engine and it is very important to assemble it properly. Lines

PARTS OF A WINDSURFING RIG

Battens:	Used for larger sails in order to give them a better shape
Boom:	Wishbone-shaped tubes; the front is attached to the mast and the back end is attached to the clew
Clamp-on:	Connects the boom to the mast
Clew:	Rear corner of the sail
Downhaul:	Pulls the sail down toward the mastfoot
Foot:	The bottom side of the sail
Head:	Top corner of the sail
Leech:	The back side of the sail
Luff:	The sail side close to the mast
Mast:	Long hollow fiberglass or aluminum tube
Mast Extension:	Part between the mast foot and mast; allows lengthening of the mast for larger sails
Mast Foot:	Connects the rig to the board. The mast foot is inserted into the mast track
Outhaul:	Pulls the sail out toward the end of the boom
Rig:	All the parts above the board's top surface
Safety Leash:	Keeps board and rig together in case mast foot separates from the board
Sail:	Has a triangular shape and a mast sleeve; comes in various sizes
Tack:	Bottom corner of the sail
Universal Joint:	Part of the mast foot that allows the rig to lean and rotate in any direction
Uphaul:	Thick line with a bungy cord that is used to lift the rig out of the water

that are not fastened correctly, a clamp-on connector that is loose, a boom that is too high or too low on the mast will make learning to windsurf very difficult and frustrating.

The sail is one of the most important parts of the rig. Sails come in various sizes and are measured in square meters or square feet. Choosing

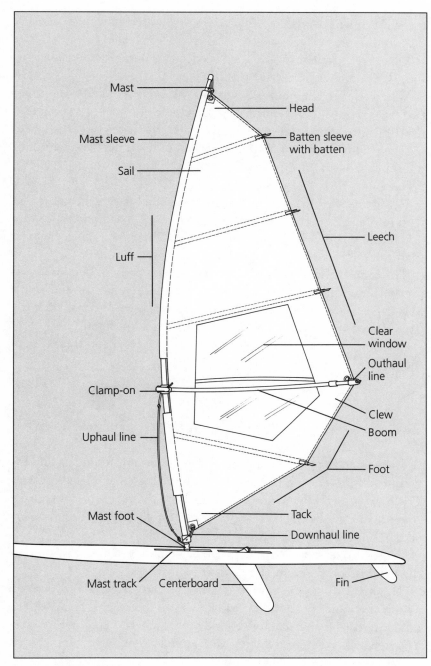

Mast

Head

Mast sleeve

Batten sleeve
with batten

Sail

Leech

Luff

Clear
window

Outhaul
line

Clamp-on

Clew

Boom

Uphaul line

Foot

Mast foot

Tack

Downhaul line

Mast track   Centerboard

Fin

Parts of a Windsurfing Rig

the sail size will depend on your size and windsurfing experience and the wind strength.

Like boards, sails can also be placed into three general categories: soft, RAF-, and camber-induced sails.

When starting to windsurf, the soft sail is preferable to the other two types of sails. It is generally more durable, has one or two battens near the head of the sail, luffs easily, and is lightweight. This makes it easier to lift the rig out of the water and to learn the basic windsurfing skills. It is an ideal sail to use in wind conditions under Beaufort Force 4.

RAF stands for rotating asymmetrical foil. This type of sail comes with full-length battens, which form a stable foil shape on the leeward side of the sail, giving the sail more power. The RAF is much heavier than the soft sail and is less forgiving during maneuvers.

The camber-induced sail also uses full-length battens, but has inserts that fit around the mast, giving it an even more efficient and stable foil shape. Camber-induced sails are more expensive, but will offer the experienced windsurfer more power, speed, and foil stability.

Let's now go on to the basic terminology used for the parts of the rig.

Wind Direction

Before you attempt to windsurf, it is very important to understand the nature and power of the wind in order to utilize its energy effectively. The way you carry the windsurfing board and the rig to the water, what size sail you use, and where and if you are able to go windsurfing are all determined by the nature of the wind.

In order to learn how the wind can be helpful, you must know where the wind is coming from and how strong it is.

The water shows some wave action. You can feel wind on your skin and in your hair. Even in light wind, you can throw grass blades or fine sand into the air and watch the wind blow them in a certain direction. You can easily determine wind direction by simply holding the rig upright and letting it swing freely.

Often it is quite easy to determine wind direction by looking at how flags are flying.

Often it is quite easy to determine wind direction by looking at how flags are flying.

Beaufort Wind Scale		
Beaufort Force Description	**Knots**	**Equivalence in Miles Per Hour**
0 Calm	0	0
1 Light Air	1–3	1–3
2 Light Breeze	4–6	4–7
3 Gentle Breeze	7–10	8–12
4 Moderate	11–15	13–18
5 Fresh	16–21	19–24
6 Strong	22–27	25–31
7 Moderate Gale	28–33	32–38
8 Fresh Gale	34–40	39–46

When learning to windsurf, avoid windsurfing in wind conditions above force 3. As windsurfing skills improve, take on stronger winds.

People who go windsurfing and ignore wind direction and wind strength will encounter nothing but difficulties. The wind governs all actions on land and on the water.

Before you begin windsurfing, use your finger to point to where the wind is coming from, and then point to where it is going. If you are uncomfortable about the place where the wind is blowing toward, do not go out. You will only drift toward the place where the wind is blowing if you are just beginning to windsurf.

Wind strength is measured using the Beaufort Wind Scale. Learn what it means and you're well on your way to being able to use the wind to your advantage.

Where to Go Windsurfing and in What Conditions

For beginners, the ideal location for windsurfing is in a lake, reservoir, or bay with a wide, sandy beach sloping into the water where windsurfing is allowed. The depth of the water should be at least chest deep.

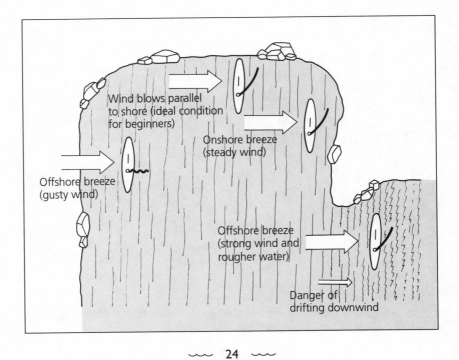

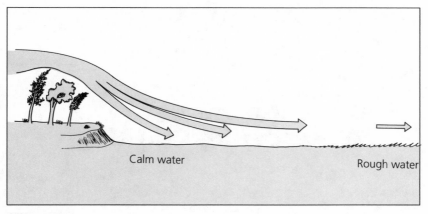

Offshore Wind

Avoid launching in areas where there are large rocks above or below the water.

Before rigging your board, make sure to determine the wind direction—whether offshore (blowing from land onto the water), or onshore (blowing from the water onto the land)—and wind strength. For an enjoyable windsurfing experience, the wind should be blowing onshore or parallel to the shore between force 1 and 3 on the Beaufort Wind Scale. Never set out in an offshore wind when you are just learning to windsurf.

Offshore winds near the shore are most often underestimated, since wind currents are slowed down and deflected by the presence of trees, houses, and shore embankments. Offshore winds can cause drifting from the safety of the shore, and tacking back to shore once you're out is difficult. *Avoid windsurfing in areas with an offshore wind if you are a beginner and not under instructional supervision.*

Once on the water, always keep an eye on the weather, especially storm warnings. Signs of an oncoming storm are thick, dark threatening clouds. While you're on the water, check the horizon once in a while for such clouds. Whether you're on a lake, river, or ocean, when a storm threatens, head immediately back to shore.

CHAPTER 2
Windsurfing Clothing

Dressing Properly

It is always a good idea for you to wear some sort of protection against the elements—water, wind, and sun. A wetsuit is one of the most important windsurfing accessories. Wetsuits protect you from hypothermia, a potentially life-threatening condition. When your body gets cold, it attempts to maintain its natural temperature of about 98.6 degrees Fahrenheit (37 degrees centigrade) by shivering. If shivering fails to maintain the body's core heat, vital organs begin to fail.

Wetsuits trap water between the suit and your body, effectively heating the trapped water and creating a layer of insulation. This helps to keep your body warm.

SUMMERWEAR

There are various types of neoprene (closed-cell rubber foam) wetsuits on the market. All wetsuits should fit snugly. The colder the climate and water temperature, the thicker your wetsuit should be. Thicknesses for wetsuits used in the summer months range from two to three millimeters and usually have a layer of nylon on both sides of the neoprene to give the suit better durability. These suits come in short-sleeved versions and in a "shorty" style.

WINTERWEAR

In cool and cold weather, four- to six-millimeter-thick smooth-skin wetsuits or dry steamers are used. They are smooth on the outside,

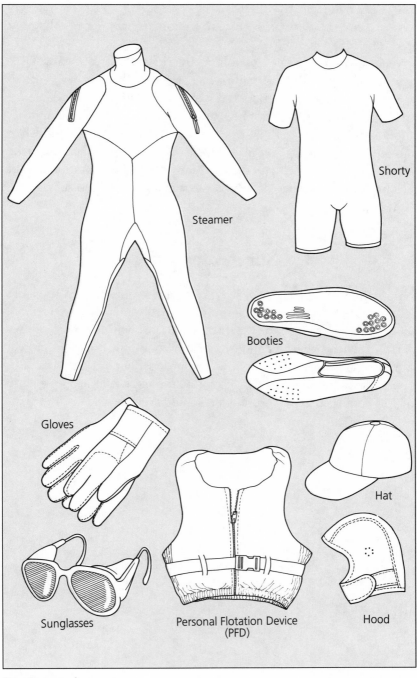

Steamer

Shorty

Booties

Gloves

Hat

Sunglasses

Personal Flotation Device
(PFD)

Hood

Dressing properly

lined with nylon on the inside. This type of suit will give you very good protection against the cold. Dry steamers are wetsuits that can keep you 75 percent dry.

Your head is the area on your body that loses the most heat, so it is very important to wear suitable head gear in cold weather. Various types of hoods, gloves, shoes, and neoprene booties are available for protection against the cold. Shoes and neoprene booties have another function: to protect your feet from injury while windsurfing and when you step off the board. They also help grip the board's surface and make it easier to operate the centerboard. Many people use flotation aids or personal flotation devices (PFDs) for extra buoyancy when they are on the water.

Sun Protection

In hot windsurfing areas, you need to protect yourself from the sun's rays. If you are not wearing a wetsuit, make sure to apply a waterproof sunscreen to exposed skin. Polarized sunglasses will protect your eyes from the glare of the sun, and a visor or a long-billed hat will protect your face. It is a good idea to check your local windsurfing school or shop to get advice on exactly which *windsurfing clothing and footgear* to wear in your specific windsurfing area and climate.

CHAPTER 3
Getting to Know Your Equipment

Rigging

Before going out windsurfing, you need to rig your sail. When rigging a sail, make sure the clamp-on connector on the boom is tightly fastened to the mast, your uphaul line is attached to your mast foot, and all lines are secured. Rigging procedures for most windsurfing boards are generally quite similar. There might be some differences between brands. When purchasing a board, you will notice that most manufacturers supply instructions detailing special rigging and board features to consider.

Follow this standard procedure.

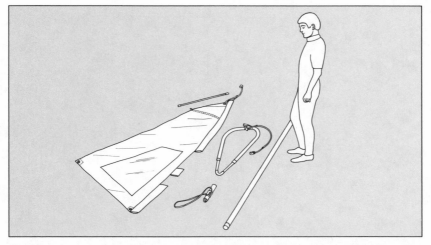

Always try to rig in an area where you have enough room and an equipment-friendly surface. The wind should be at your back and the parts of the rig to leeward.

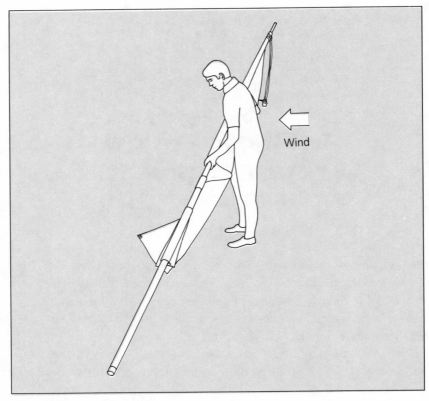

Slide the mast into the mast sleeve.

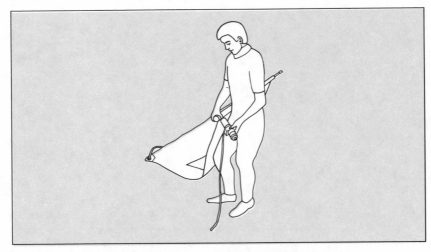

Insert the mast foot into the mast, making sure there is no dirt in the mast.

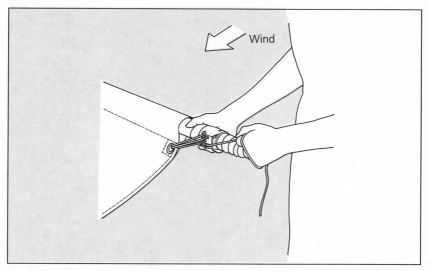

Attach the downhaul to the tack of the sail and go through the pulley system twice, then apply a little tension.

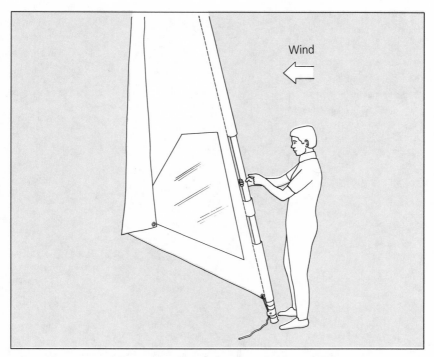

Lift the mast and decide where you want to attach the boom. Boom height should be between chest and shoulder high.

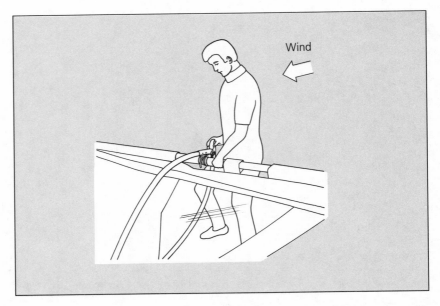

Wind

Lay down the mast and sail and attach the clamp-on boom to the mast. The uphaul is attached to the clamp-on connector and is hanging down toward the mast foot. Attach the uphaul to the mast foot with a bungee cord.

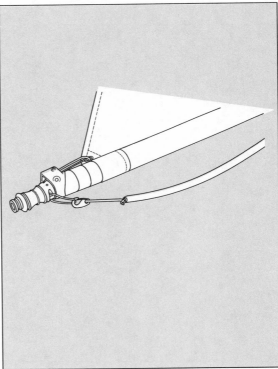

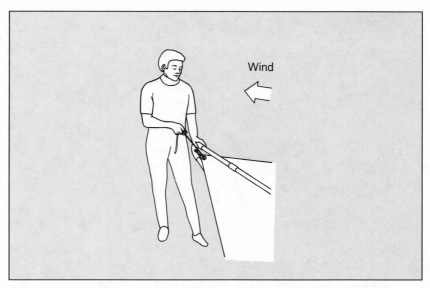

If you have an adjustable boom, adjust it to fit the sail. Then pull the sail out with the outhaul line and go through the cleat to fasten it off.

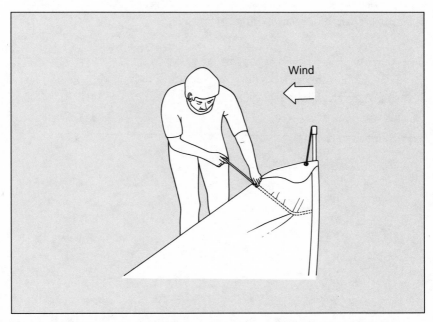

If your sail has battens, insert them now and secure them with their tension system.

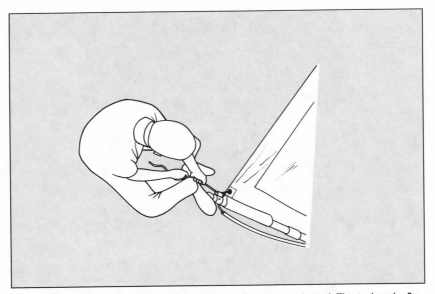

Then apply tension to the downhaul. Remove all the wrinkles in the sail. This is done by fine-tuning the sail with the downhaul and uphaul. If your sail has any vertical creases, simply tighten the outhaul or loosen the downhaul. If the sail has any horizontal creases running from the clew to the luff, simply loosen the outhaul or tighten the downhaul. Fasten all lines securely in the manner described by the rig's manufacturer.

Always attach the rig to your board immediately after rigging. This will ensure that your rig will not be blown away if wind conditions pick up.

Derigging

Derigging is accomplished by first releasing batten tension. Then you slowly release the downhaul tension, and finally the outhaul tension. Continue derigging in the reverse order of how the windsurfer was rigged. Sails are generally rolled up after use and stored in a sailbag. It is always a good idea to rinse your equipment in order to remove dirt after a day of windsurfing. The sail should be dry when stored in a sailbag.

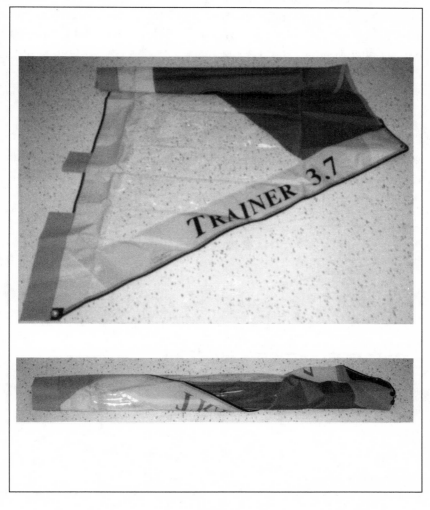

Equipment-Handling Techniques

In order to begin windsurfing successfully, it's important to master some basic equipment-handling techniques first. Once you're comfortable with the rig assembly, you'll be able to progress to various techniques associated with the board itself.

The majority of problems the beginning windsurfer has are due to the rig, because of its unusual ability to rotate on its mast foot.

Practice carrying your rig to various points in the rigging area and practice some land exercises with it to improve and facilitate your equipment-handling skills. You need to become familiar with the rig, its weight, how it reacts in the wind, and how to balance it on the mast foot before attempting to go out into the water. Make sure you have enough room in your rigging area to practice the upcoming drills in light wind conditions.

Carrying Your Rig to the Water

When you begin windsurfing for real, you'll always start by placing your rig into the water before the board. This is done because the rig will not drift away from you as fast as the board will.

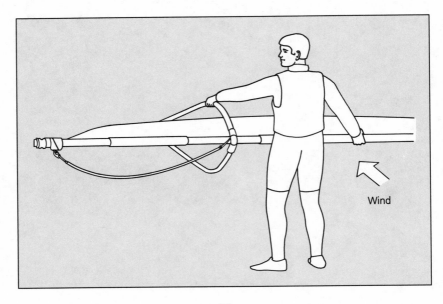

Wind

When carrying your rig away from the wind, make sure that the clamp-on connector is pointed toward the wind. Stand with your back to the wind in front of the mast and place one hand on the mast above the boom and lift the rig in order to plant the mast foot in the ground. Place your other hand on the boom and lift the rig off the ground, keeping it at a 90-degree angle to the wind as you walk it to the water.

Carrying a Rig into the Wind

When you're carrying your rig into the wind, the rig should be positioned on the ground with its clamp-on connector pointed into the wind.

Place one hand on the mast above the boom, lift the rig, and plant the mast foot in the ground. Reach underneath the rig with your other hand and grab the boom to lift the rig over your head.

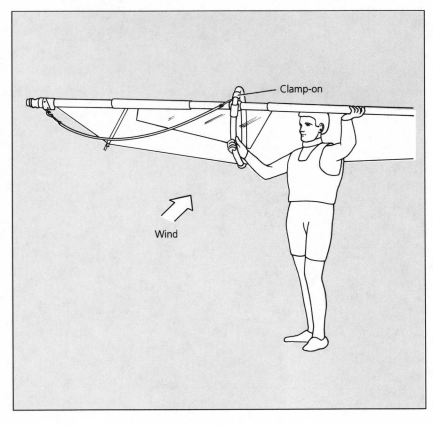

Rig Exercises on Land

After you've practiced the two carrying methods for the rig, it's time to become more familiar with the rig and how it rotates on its mast foot. Here are a few exercises that will help in learning how to control the rig in the wind. These exercises should be practiced in light to gentle breezes—Beaufort Wind Scale 1, 2, or 3.

Position your rig to leeward (downwind) so the clamp-on connector is pointing into the wind. Place one foot on the mast foot to anchor it and lift the rig by grabbing the mast just above the boom. Then grab the mast with both hands just below the boom and pause. If there is any wind at all, the rig will catch the wind and point in the direction it's blowing.

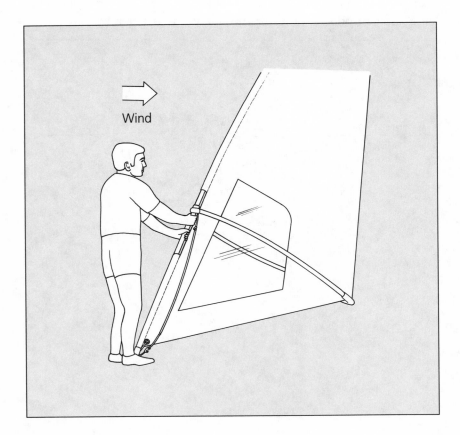

Wind

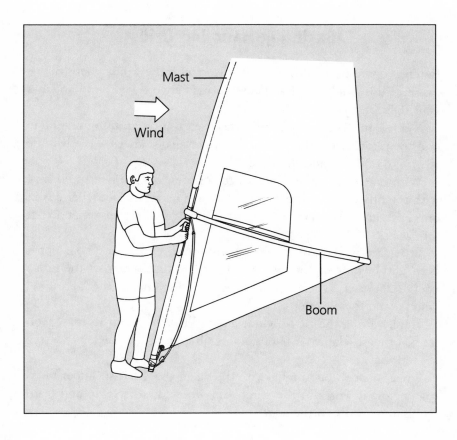

Basic Rig-Handling Drills

Extend your arms to allow the rig to lean with the wind. Then try this exercise, using only one hand, alternating between your left hand and your right on the mast.

Next, lean the rig to one side and then the other, using one hand and then using the other hand. Then bend your knees while leaning the rig to one side and then the other.

With one foot on the mast foot to continue anchoring it, step back with the other foot so there is a distance of about two feet. Bend your arm back until the mast touches your shoulder and then extend your arm again.

Bring the mast farther back to windward, by rotating your upper body and by moving the mast hand to windward. Then let the rig go back to leeward. Repeat several times and also change the mast hand when doing these exercises.

Finally, bring the rig to windward and balance it on its mast foot, let go of mast, clap your hands, and grab mast again. Repeat this step several times.

Once you feel comfortable with the rig and have a basic understanding of how it works in the wind, you are ready to suit up and learn windsurfing skills on the water.

CHAPTER 4
Handling Drills and Theory

Carrying Your Board

Flip your board on its side with the top surface facing you. Insert the centerboard. Place one hand on the mast foot or into the mast track. Place your other hand into the centerboard well and carry it down to the shore. Place your board close to the water. Point the bow of the board toward the water with the bottom surface of the board up. This will prevent damage to the fin.

If you are windsurfing with a friend, it is easier to carry each board down to the shore together. Flip the board on its side with the top surface facing you. One person should grab the bow of the board while the other grabs the stern.

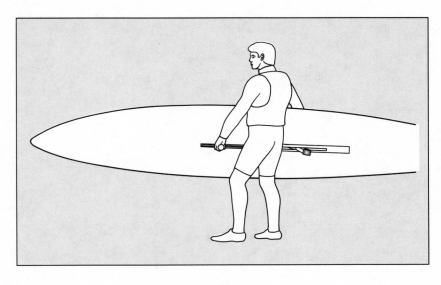

Paddling and Balancing Exercises

Paddling and balancing exercises will help you become familiar with the area to be windsurfed, the board, and wind conditions. The following exercises should be practiced in a safe windsurfing environment with others nearby.

Getting onto the board is quite easy: In chest-deep water, place your hands on each side of the centerboard well. Paddle with both feet to lift body higher out of the water and slide onto the board while rotating your body so that both feet end up on the board. Try these exercises and master them before going windsurfing.

- Paddle with both hands.
- Paddle with alternating hands.
- Stop the board by paddling in reverse with both hands.
- Paddle to various points of the windsurfing area.
- Practice turning your board 360 degrees in both directions.
- Practice getting off the board, flipping it over, and then getting back on.

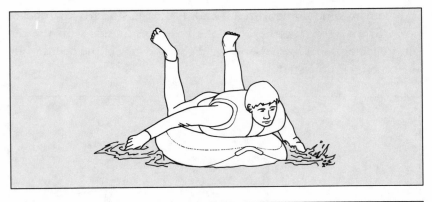

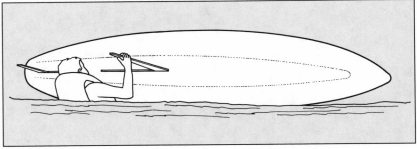

BALANCING

Because it is so important for you to be able to balance on your board while standing, it is a good idea to practice the exercises without the rig attached. The following balancing exercises will teach you how the board reacts when stood on and should be practiced in at least shoulder-deep water. If you fall off the board, remember to come up with your arms first to protect your head from hitting the board.

- Kneeling on the board, place hands left and right of centerboard, push yourself up, and stand up straight. It is very important to keep your weight over the centerline of the board.

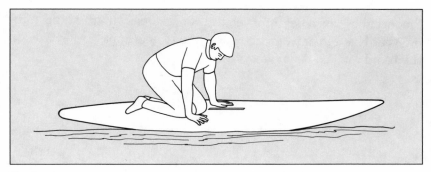

Kneeling

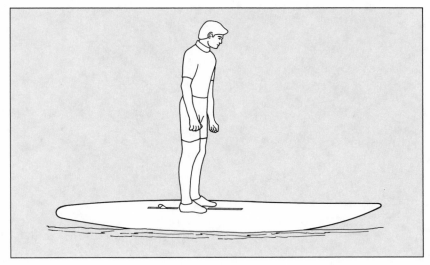

Standing

- Apply slight pressure to the rail areas, rocking the board.
- Drop back to your knees and stand up on the board (repeat this several times).
- With small steps move slowly toward the bow and then the stern.
- Do quarter-turns on your board.
- Try to stand on one leg, then the other for a short period.
- Jump into the water and come up with your arms outstretched first. Remember always to swim immediately to your board after a fall. Think of it as your island of safety.
- Practice these exercises first with the centerboard down and then with it up.
- If you start drifting off, simply paddle back to your starting point.

Practice these exercises until you feel comfortable with paddling, turning your board in any direction, and until you are able to stand up on the board for a good amount of time.

Windsurfing Terms

The majority of windsurfing terms come from the sailing community. When windsurfing, we can sail various courses, which are called *points of sail*.

- *Close-hauled* means you are windsurfing upwind approximately 45 degrees to the true wind.
- *Beam reach* is a course 90 degrees to the wind.
- *Broad reach* is a course between beam reach and a run.
- *Run* is windsurfing directly downwind.

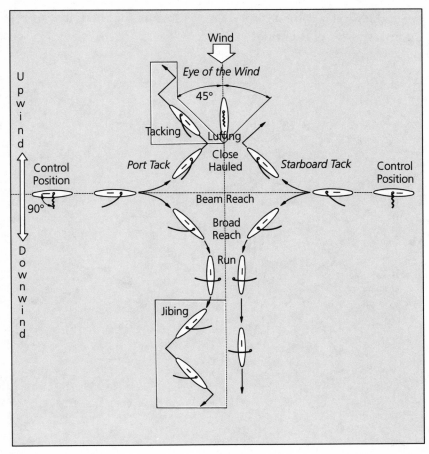

Points of Sail

It is important for you to understand that you cannot windsurf directly into the wind. If you windsurf directly into the *eye of the wind*, your sail will start luffing and you will stop moving forward.

When windsurfing, you are either on a *port tack* or a *starboard tack*. When you are windsurfing on a port tack, you are standing on the port side, the side where the wind is blowing over.

When you are windsurfing on a starboard tack, you are standing on the starboard side where the wind is blowing over.

There is an easy way for you to know which tack you are on. All you need to do is look at your hands on the boom. If your right hand is closer to the mast, then you are on a starboard tack; if your left hand is closer to the mast, you are on a port tack.

A *tack* is a turn where the front of the windsurfer passes through the eye of the wind; a *jibe* is a turn where the back of the windsurfer passes through the eye of the wind.

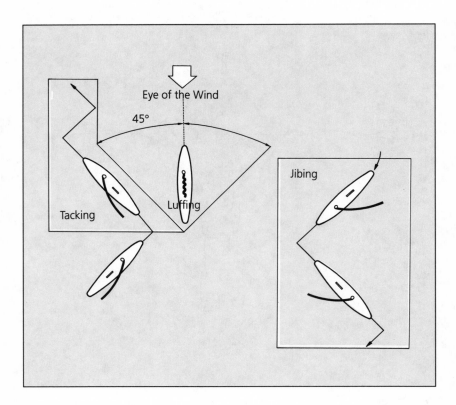

The wind blows from one direction at a time. When an object is closer to the source of the wind, we use the term *windward* or upwind. An object farther away from the source of the wind is *leeward* or downwind.

Heading up means to steer the windsurfer to the source of the wind (toward windward), whereas *bearing off* means steering the windsurfer away from the wind (toward leeward).

Sheeting in or trimming the sail means pulling the sail in so that it fills with air. *Sheeting out* means letting the sail out so that the sail's power is reduced.

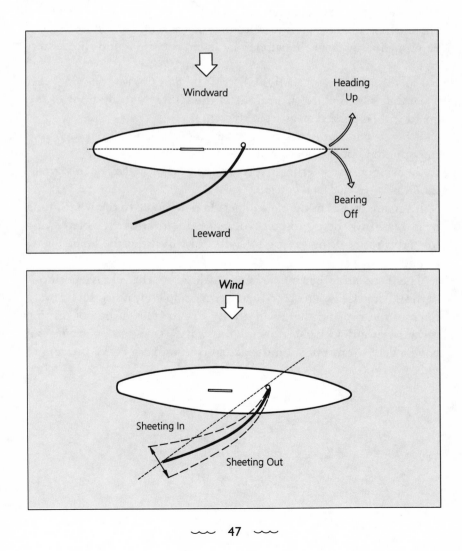

How You Steer Your Windsurfing Board

The sum of all the forces (wind) acting on the sail can be said to act on one point only. This point is called the *center of effort* (CE).

This force in the sail would simply push you sideways if there weren't any resistance offered by the centerboard, fin, and all other submerged parts on your board. The centerboard represents the *center of lateral resistance* (CLR). Your windsurfing board will move in a straight line if the two forces are aligned with each other. That means that the CE is **aligned** with the CLR.

Knowing this explains how the board can be steered if we *shift* the CE (rig) *toward the back and leeward*. The back of the windsurfer will be pushed away from the wind. The board pivots around the centerboard.

On the other hand, if the CE (rig) is *shifted toward the front and windward*, which places it in front of the CLR, then the front of the board will be pushed away from the wind.

When the front or back of the board is pushed away from the wind, the other end of the board will head toward the wind.

Remember that steering involves *shifting the rig to the front and windward, or to the back and leeward.*

If you are on a run, the rig will be at a right angle to the windsurfing board. Shifting the rig to port will make the front of the board swing to starboard. Shifting the rig to starboard will make the board swing to port.

There are also other influences in addition to the relative positions of the CE and CLR. The board can never completely resist the sideways force of the rig, and there will always be a certain degree of drifting toward leeward. Other factors such as waves, tides, and currents can have a very strong effect on the actual course that a board is trying to sail.

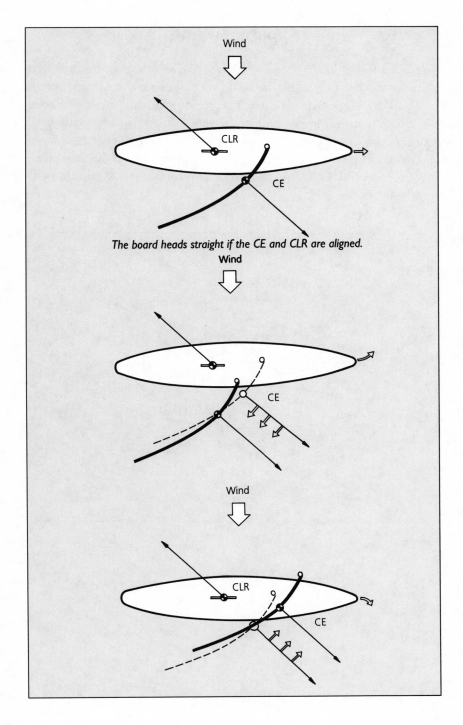

The board heads straight if the CE and CLR are aligned.

Apparent Wind

True wind is wind that blows when you are standing on land. When you are out windsurfing and the board starts moving through the water, an equal and "opposite" wind is felt due to the windsurfer's forward motion. When running or riding a bicycle, you can also feel this wind coming from directly ahead. This wind is called *created wind*, or more plainly, wind due to board speed. The combination of the true wind and created wind results in *apparent wind*, which is the wind that pulls your board forward.

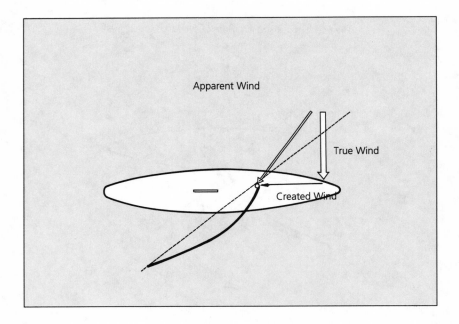

How a Sail Works

On a beam reach, close-hauled, or broad reach course, the apparent wind will blow across the leading edge of the sail at a small angle (angle of attack).

The air flow, which is divided by the mast and sail, streams along the sail to windward and leeward before merging again at the leech of the sail. On the leeward side, the air is diverted by the curvature of the sail and has to travel farther, and thus faster. This causes a difference

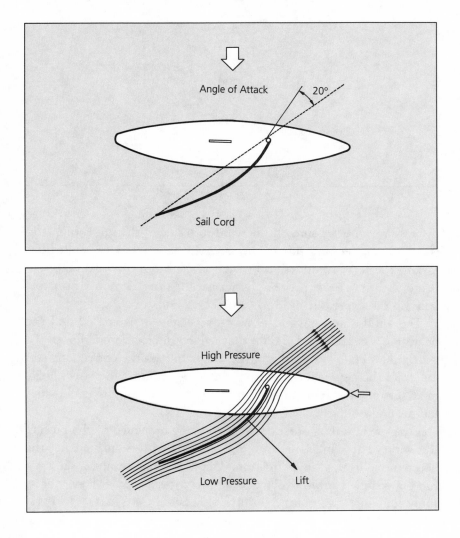

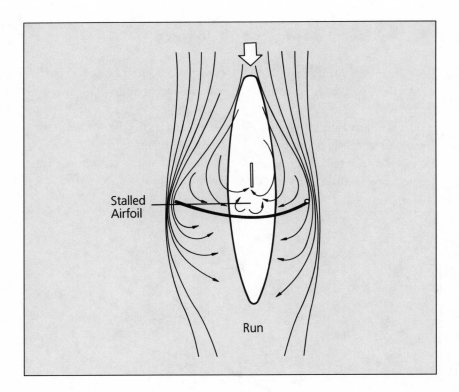

Stalled Airfoil

Run

in pressure. The pressure on the windward side of the sail is high and is low on the leeward side of the sail. The sail material is pulled out toward the leeward direction by suction. The sail lifts and takes the board with it. This theory of physics is called the Bernoulli principle and was discovered in 1738 by Daniel Bernoulli.

The windsurfing sail functions only because it is curved and the board has a centerboard and fin that will counteract lateral forces. To get the best performance out of the sail, trim it to the correct angle of attack to the apparent wind. It is easy to determine the correct angle of attack; you just need to sheet in the sail to the point where it stops luffing, and no farther.

When windsurfing on a run, you are being propelled by the push of the wind. The wind is pushing on one side of the sail, making the board move in the same direction. The flow of air around a sail on a run has a stalled airfoil which does not have a smooth air flow over its surface, making this point of sail the slowest.

CHAPTER 5
Setting Out

Lifting the Rig Out of the Water

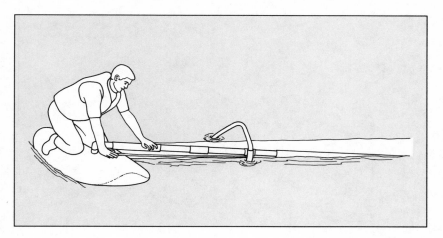

Before lifting the rig out of the water, make sure that the mast foot is securely attached to the board. The rig should be positioned on the leeward side and the mast should be at a 90-degree angle to the board. The bow of the board is pointing toward the water.

Grasp the uphaul at the bottom and slide onto the board with knees to the left and right of the mast foot. Then place one hand on the mast and one on the board. Push yourself up holding onto the uphaul. Your feet should still be left and right of the mast foot, shoulder width apart, on the centerline of the board. Bend your knees and make your back as straight as possible. The taller you are, the wider your stance should be on the board.

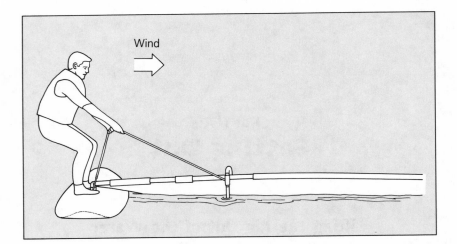

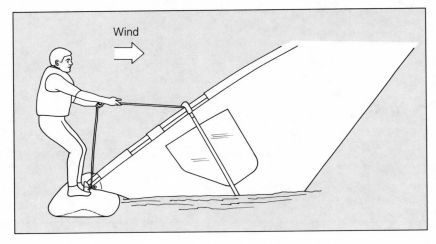

At this point, make sure that the mast is at a 90-degree angle to the board. If the rig is not at a right angle, simply lean the rig toward the board's bow or the stern to position it correctly for lifting.

With both hands on the uphaul, lift the rig out of the water by straightening your legs and bending them again, and at the same time pulling the uphaul hand-over-hand upward until you can grab the mast. Hold the mast with both hands just below the boom. Make sure you lift the rig with your leg muscles rather than with your back. You will notice that once the water has drained off the sail, the rig lifts relatively easily out of the water. Grab the mast with both hands just below the boom to get into the *control position*.

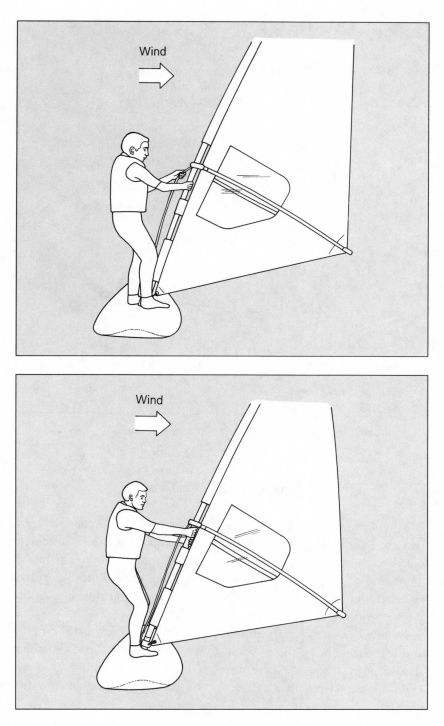

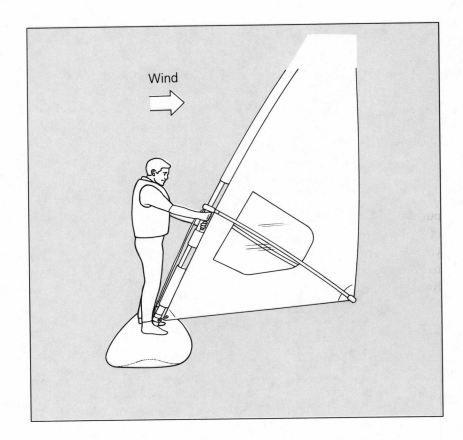

Getting Under Way

With your knees slightly bent, your back straight, and your arms extended, look at the end of the boom to check that the boom end is out of the water and that the rig is at a 90-degree angle to the board. The wind should be at your back. If you feel uncomfortable in this position and begin to lose your balance, simply drop the rig into the water, get down on your knees, and start all over.

In case the rig falls to windward of the board, slowly lift the rig up and leave the end of the boom in the water. By doing this, the board should slowly turn until the rig is again on the leeward side of the board. You can then lift the rig out of the water and get into the control position.

Falling

Falling off the board is an inevitable part of windsurfing. You will not be able to improve your windsurfing skills without falling into the water.

To avoid damaging your rig and injuring yourself, try to fall into the water opposite of where the rig is, and avoid falling on the board. If the rig does fall on top of you and you find yourself underneath the sail, stay calm. Lift your hands above your head and feel your way to the leech or luff of the sail, then get out from underneath the rig and pull yourself onto the board. It is always a good idea to come up out of the water with your hands and arms first, in order to avoid hitting your head on some part of the rig. Remember to swim back immediately to your board after falling; otherwise, it may drift away and you will have to swim even farther to reach it.

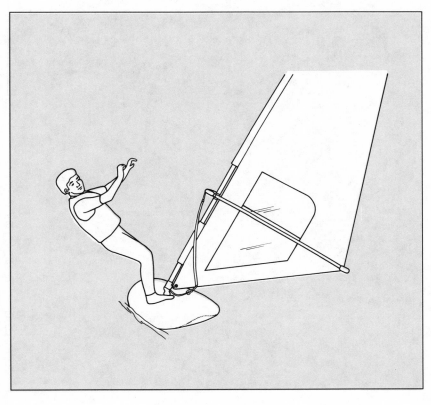

Exercise: Leaning the Rig to the Bow and Stern

Simply by leaning the rig slowly to the bow or stern of the board, you will be able to position the board and maintain the control position. Practice leaning the rig and maintaining the control position until you feel comfortable with it. It is important that your arms be extended, your back straight, and your knees slightly bent, and that the clew is out of the water.

180-Degree Turn

Now that you understand how to get into the control position, the next skill to learn is how to turn your board around so it points in the opposite direction. Every time you turn your board around, remember to check the surrounding area for any obstacles and other windsurfers.

You need to understand that the board's position changes according to how much you lean the rig, and that the board can be turned in any direction.

Turning the bow away from the wind will push you downwind during a turn. Turning the bow through the eye of the wind will keep you upwind. In the beginning, you should practice the 180-degree turn leaning the rig toward the stern of the board to stay upwind. In your particular windsurfing area you should practice leaning your rig to the bow and stern, and the 180-degree turn, until you are able to maintain your position by just leaning the rig and turning your board.

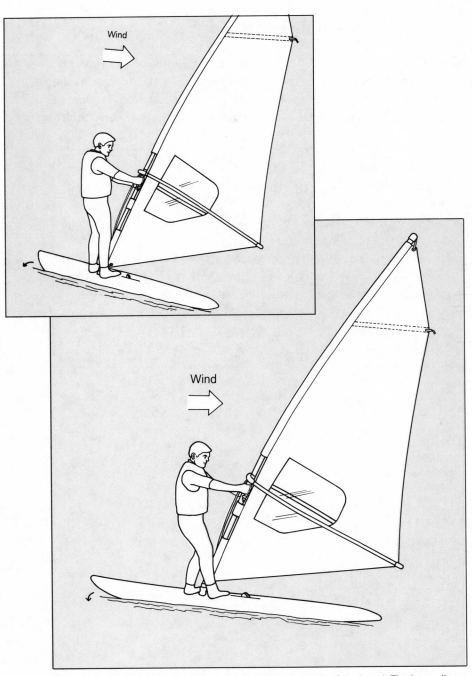

From the control position, slowly lean the rig toward the back of the board. The bow will turn into the wind.

Keep your arms extended, your back straight, and the rig directly in front of you.

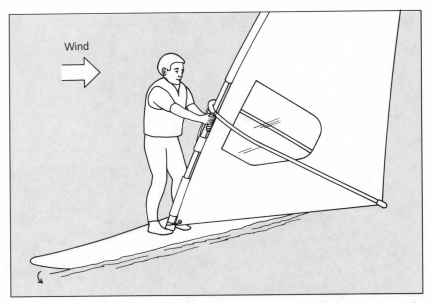

Follow the rig's direction with tiny steps around the mast foot, while keeping your eyes on the end of the boom. Keep your toes pointed in that direction. Remember to lean first and then slowly move around the mast to the front of the board. Keep your toes pointed toward the end of the boom.

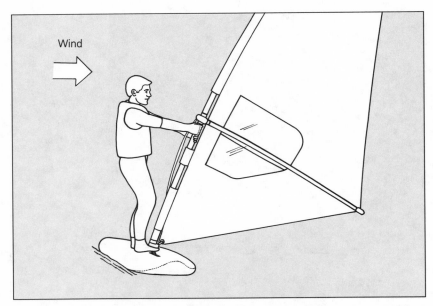

Once the bow of the board has gone through the eye of the wind, continue turning until you have reached a new control position, and therefore completed a 180-degree turn.

The Starting Position

Now that you know how to lean your rig to the bow and stern, and are also able to do 180-degree turns, try practicing the starting position.

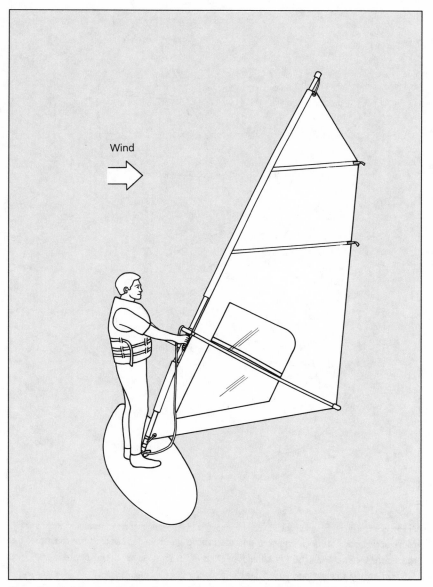

Wind

From the control position, drop the hand closest to the stern to your side.

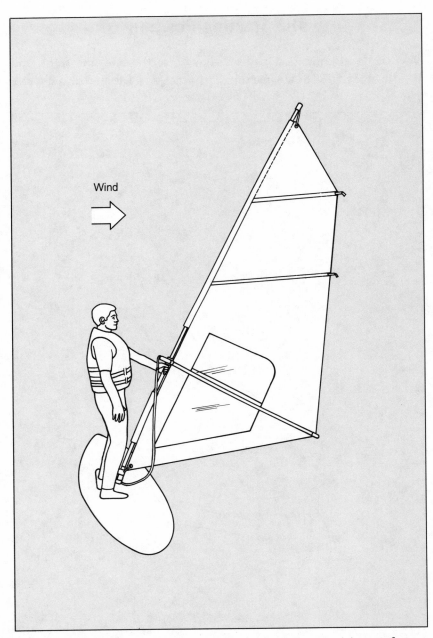

Wind

Move your back foot back one step and then move the front foot behind the mast foot onto the board's centerline. The rig should be at a 90-degree angle to the board. Finally, your forward arm is straight and your knees are slightly bent.

Getting into the Windsurfing Position

From the starting position, look to the front and check area around you for obstacles.

Bring your rig to the windward side by rotating your upper body windward and shifting your weight to the back foot. Position your upper body parallel to the sail, and balance the rig on the mast foot so it is on a 90-degree angle to the board.

Look through the window of the sail and rotate your front foot toward the bow. Place your trim hand (your back hand) on the boom. Place your mast hand (front hand) on the boom (in areas with gusty wind conditions, keep the mast hand on the mast and place mast hand on boom after getting into the windsurfing position). Hands should be placed shoulder-width apart on the boom and elbows should be aimed downward.

Rotate upper body and rig. Stop rotating as soon as you see the front of the board and the sail stops luffing.

It is very important that you understand all these steps—starting and getting into the windsurfing position. These are very important skills to master at this level. You should be able to recite the sequence of movements orally. (This is a good way to check your understanding of starting and getting into the windsurfing position. Also remember that the pressure on the rig lessens when the trim hand eases or loosens up on the rig.)

Windsurfing Position

In the windsurfing position, your mast should be as vertical as possible and you should be looking past the bow of your board. Your boom should be parallel to the board.

In winds under force 3 on the Beaufort Wind Scale, point your elbows down and position both hands approximately shoulder-width apart on the boom. Use an overhand grip, with your palms gripping the boom from the top. Your upper body should be straight with your knees slightly bent to distribute weight on both feet evenly. Place your front foot directly behind the mast foot and your back foot on top of the centerboard well.

As soon as you get into the windsurfing position, you will notice the force of the wind in your sail. Hold on to your mast hand and trim hand and you will be windsurfing!

If you feel as if you are falling backward, bend your knees immediately and sheet in your sail with the trim hand. Before falling in, it is better to push your rig over to the leeward side of your board, then get down on your knees and start lifting the rig out of the water again.

If you feel as if you are being pulled forward, simply sheet out with your trim hand to reduce the force. And if you still feel uncomfortable in the windsurfing position, go back to the starting position and try again.

Returning to the Control Position

To return to the control position, simply release your trim hand and immediately extend your mast hand for stability. Now move back into the control position. At this point, practice starting, getting into the windsurfing position, going back to the control position, and making 180-degree turns a number of times, until comfortable with all of these maneuvers.

Stopping the Windsurfing Board

When you are windsurfing and want to stop the board's forward motion, get into the control position.

    If you are returning to shore, use the control position technique or place your mast hand on the mast, then slide your mast hand down approximately one foot below the boom while at the same time bending your knees. Grab the foot of your sail and release the mast hand. Always make sure to check the area around you (especially the leeward side for obstacles and people). Let your mast hit the water and the board will stop moving. Always remember to get off the board slowly. At this point, to take your equipment out of the water, remove the mast foot and safety line. Carry your board back to shore and then go back to retrieve the rig from the water.

Steering the Windsurfing Board

In order to windsurf upwind or downwind, you need to be able to steer your board. If you want to windsurf in the direction of the wind (upwind) you have to sometimes change direction. (The sailing term for this change in direction in relation to the wind is *heading up*.)

Check the area around you then move your weight to the front foot, and slowly shift your rig to the back and leeward of your board by extending the trim hand and keeping the mast hand close to our body.

To stop the turning motion, simply return to the windsurfing position by bringing your boom parallel to the board, looking to the front, and keeping your elbows down.

To windsurf in the direction away from the wind (downwind) prac-

tice the following steps. (The sailing term for this change in direction in relation to the wind is *bearing off*.)

Check the area around you and move your weight to the back foot. Then slowly shift your rig to the front and windward of the board, by extending the mast hand and keeping the trim hand close to your body.

To stop the turning motion, simply return to the windsurfing position again; bring the boom parallel to the board, look to the front, and keep your elbows pointed down.

Practice windsurfing an S-shaped course to make sure that you are comfortable with these maneuvers. Remember to keep your knees slightly bent for optimum control.

Windsurfing directly into the eye of the wind is impossible; if your sail starts luffing, you either have to bear off or do a 180-degree turn.

Tacking

The tack is a turn where the bow of the board passes through the eye of the wind and causes a change in the rig's side of travel. A series of tacks is called tacking. Use the same technique as for making a 180-degree turn, where the rig passes over the stern of the board. A tack is more efficient than a 180-degree turn. We lose less ground by tacking to windward.

As you've learned by now, it is impossible to sail directly into the eye of the wind. In order to reach a point in a windsurfing area that is to windward it is necessary to windsurf in a zigzag course.

Windsurf on a close-hauled course and check area around you (1), before making the turn. Move your mast hand to the mast just below the boom and shift your rig to the back and leeward (2). Your board will turn more toward windward at this time. Move your front foot in front of mast, toes pointed toward the stern of the board (3). Keep your back straight and mast close to your body.

The luffing of the sail should be recognized as the signal for the trim hand to slide to the mast, and to begin stepping around it.

When the bow of your board passes through the eye of the wind, go before the mast, by sliding the trim hand toward the mast and grasping it (4). Keep arms straight, knees slightly bent, back as straight as possible, and lean the rig until you have reached new control position, using small steps (5 and 6).

Now get back to the windsurfing position and practice more tacks.

The Tack

Jibing

The jibe is a turn where the stern of the board passes through the eye of the wind and causes the rig to change sides. A series of jibes is called jibing. A jibe draws on the same techniques as used for the 180-degree turn, where the rig passes over the bow of the board.

You should be windsurfing on a beam reach before you jibe. Check the area around you for other windsurfers or obstacles (1).

Shift your rig to the front and windward to initiate the jibe (2).

When your board turns away from the wind, adjust rig perpendicular to the wind. At this point the wind is directly behind your back. (If you continue windsurfing downwind, you will be on a run.) Position your feet on either side of the centerboard well (3).

Continue the jibe by sliding your front foot back and by sliding your back foot forward (4). Release your trim hand and let the rig swing over the bow (5), move your trim hand to mast and let the rig swing over the bow. Get into the starting position and assume the windsurfing position (6).

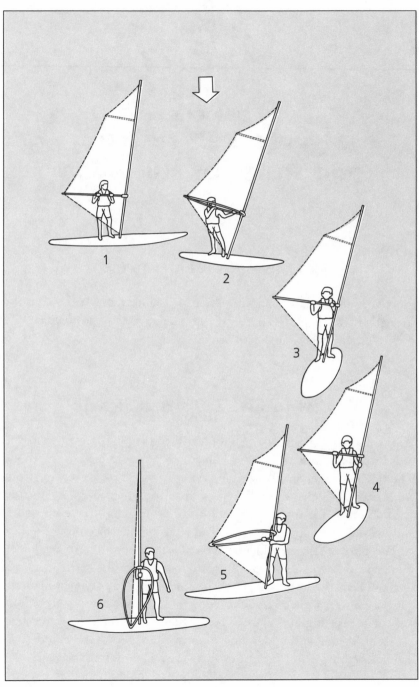

The Jibe

CHAPTER 6
Signals, Self-Rescue, and Rules of the Road

In Case of an Emergency

A situation just may come up when you simply may not have the strength to get back to shore. Just remember this basic rule: Always stay calm, and most important, *stay on your board*.

How to Give a Distress Signal

A distress signal has to be given clearly and be sufficiently visible in order to start a rescue mission immediately. There are two methods. The first one is especially visible and easy to perform even in strong wind and turbulent water: Stand or kneel on your board, balance by holding on to the uphaul line; with the other hand, wave a brightly colored object such as a life jacket in slow circular motions.

The second distress signal is given as follows: From a sitting, kneeling, or standing position move your outstretched arms (from the side of your body) slowly up and down. Unfortunately, this type of signaling cannot be seen for a great distance because wave activity will hide it. However, repeat giving signals until you are reasonably sure that help is on the way. Don't, under any circumstances, get off the board. Cold water can draw heat from the body twenty times faster than air.

Should you ever see someone signaling for help, immediately notify authorities if you can't attempt the rescue yourself.

Self-Rescue Techniques

If the wind dies down or if something breaks, use these methods to return to shore. This first method described can be used in light to moderate wind conditions. From a sitting position release your mast foot from the board. Remove the battens from the sail and place them underneath yourself and later slide them into the rolled-up sail. Remove the boom by releasing the outhaul and clamp-on, and place it

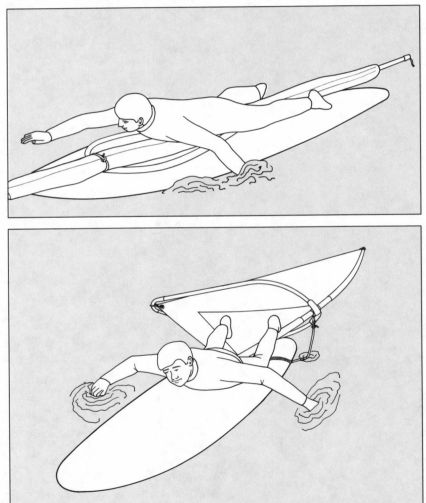

Simply set the rig down and lay it over the bow or stern if you run into any difficulties while windsurfing.

on top of the board. Now roll up the sail tightly and attach the boom to the mast with your uphaul and outhaul lines. Lay the rig on your board and paddle back to shore (see top illustration on page 82).

If there is no wind, simply pull the rig over the stern of your board, hold the rig down on the board with your feet, and paddle back to shore (see bottom illustration on page 82).

Basic Rules of the Road

"Rules of the road" is the nautical phrase that explains who has the right-of-way on the water. It is your responsibility to learn these rules. The general tenets are to be *cautious and respectful of others* on the water, and to avoid collisions.

All vessels have to conduct themselves in such a way that traffic can proceed safely and with ease. No vessel may damage, endanger, or (except in unavoidable circumstances) inconvenience or obstruct another vessel. All the precautionary measures appropriate to the prevailing circumstances and conditions must be considered.

The most commonly used rules are those which apply when you are windsurfing among other sailboats and other windsurfing boards. These rules are grouped into three general categories:

WINDSURFING BOARDS THAT CONVERGE WHILE ON OPPOSITE TACKS (SAILS OF BOARDS ON OPPOSITE SITES)

When you are windsurfing and your sail is off to your right (your starboard side), the wind is coming across your port side, you are sailing a *port tack*. You are said to be windsurfing a *starboard tack* when the wind is coming across your starboard side (your sail is off to port).

A board on *starboard tack* has right-of-way over a board on *port tack*. This is shown clearly in the top illustration on page 84: B has right-of-way.

WINDSURFING BOARDS ON THE SAME TACK CONVERGING

The *leeward* board has right-of-way over *windward* board. B has right-of-way (see bottom illustration on page 84).

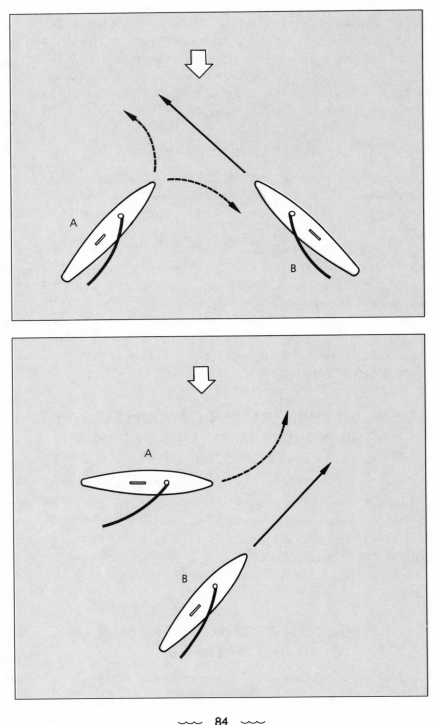

WINDSURFING BOARDS OF DIFFERENT SPEEDS
WINDSURFING ALONG THE SAME COURSE

The *overtaking* board *keeps clear*.

This means that the faster board must find another course for passing the slower board. This new course must not hinder the sailing conditions (that is, steal any air from) the slower windsurfing board. A has the right-of-way.

Other important rules apply when a windsurfing board is converging on the same course as powerboats. The first of these rules is: *Motorized vehicles* must yield to all sailing craft.

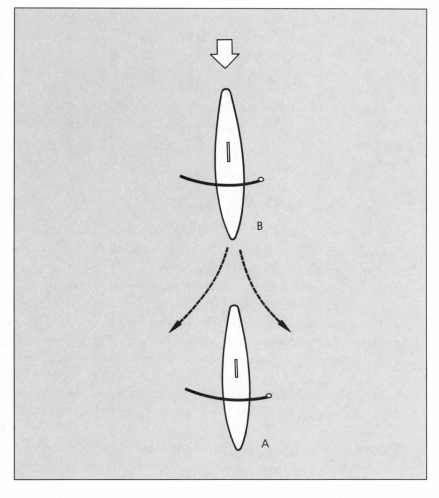

However, if the motorized vehicle is a ferry or other commercial vessel, the following rule applies: *Commercial vessels* have *unconditional right-of-way*. Windsurfing boards should keep well clear of these vessels at all times.

Here is a final rule: Windsurfing boards, sailboats, and powerboats must stay clear of manually powered vessels. This includes paddle and row boats, canoes, and air mattresses. Of course, you must always use caution around swimmers and divers.

Note: Certain Rules and regulations may vary from state to state. Be sure to check with your local or regional boating authority or U.S. Coast Guard.

Weather

Before you go windsurfing, it is very important to check the weather and wind conditions in your windsurfing area. You can do this by listening to the weather report on TV or reading your local newspaper. VHF weatherband radios are also available. They give boaters weather updates on a regular basis concerning windstrength, tides, and conditions in general.

LAND AND SEA BREEZES

The effect of the sun each day on land and water creates a wind system. These are local winds of short duration caused because land is heated much more quickly by the sun than is water.

In the early morning, it takes a little while for heat from the sun to take effect, but soon the warm air over the land, which is heated more quickly, starts to rise and a small low-pressure area is formed. This air flows from over the cooler water toward land. This is the sea breeze that blows toward the shore. When the general weather situation is relatively stable, you can expect a sea breeze to start between ten o'clock and noon on sunny days. The sea breeze drops at sunset, and you can often see an area of smooth water spreading gradually offshore in the evening.

The process is reversed at night. Unlike the water, land cools very quickly at sunset. Air rises above the now warmer water, and the local low pressure area formed draws in cooled air from the land. A nightly land breeze starts to blow offshore just as reliably as the sea breeze.

These winds occur relatively constantly all along the coasts, but inland waters have to be of a certain size to generate a worthwhile wind. When they do occur, they are usually much stronger than those found on the coast. Woods, open land, and varying heights of land nearby impede or accentuate the thermal effect. In particular, the fric-

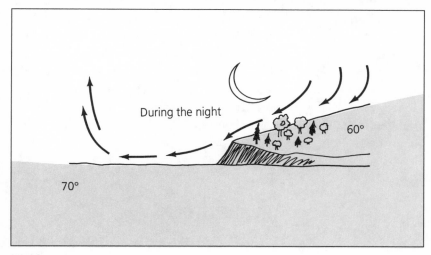

During the night

60°

70°

Land Breeze

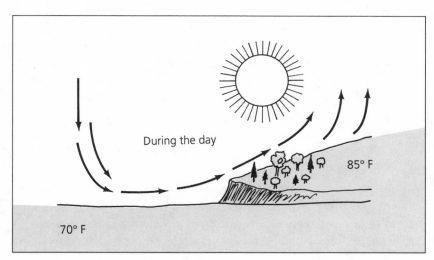

During the day

85° F

70° F

Sea Breeze

tion arising from the rough surface of the land affects the wind. There is little frictional resistance from the open sea, even when waves are high, and the wind stays relatively steady, but inland the surface is rarely level because of topographic factors like low hills or a range of moderately high mountains. Friction basically reduces the speed of the wind, but the wind also becomes gusty.

For your safety, you must find out about local wind conditions and especially know what the weather and wind will be doing the day you are windsurfing. When you visit a new windsurfing area, get advice from local windsurfers or sailors concerning the sailing area, and the weather conditions that typically prevail in that specific area.

Apart from official warnings, you must always keep an eye on the weather, especially on inland bodies of water where the situation can change quickly. Deterioration can almost always be anticipated by studying cloud formation, so check frequently across the horizon for signs of impending bad weather.

THUNDERSTORMS

A thunderstorm develops when high temperatures collide with a very humid atmosphere. Heat causes air to rise very rapidly and it can shoot upward to where it cools. The moisture in the air quickly condenses, and drops of water or ice, which are too heavy to be supported by the rising air, fall to the ground as thunder, rain, or hail. All this is accompanied by violent gusts. The static electricity generated as moisture condenses is discharged as lightning, which travels between clouds or down to earth. It is easy to see the formation of a thunderstorm with its dark tower of clouds reaching skyward. When thick cumulus clouds concentrate at one point on the horizon and start to soar upward, with an anvil-shaped cap (cumulonimbus) spreading sideways, you know there will soon be a thunderstorm.

Thunder areas can persist for some days with local storms popping up here and there. A big disturbance can completely knock out the prevailing pressure-generated wind over a wide area. Features of this condition are flat calms, alternating winds from any direction, and violent, brief storms that seldom last more than an hour or two.

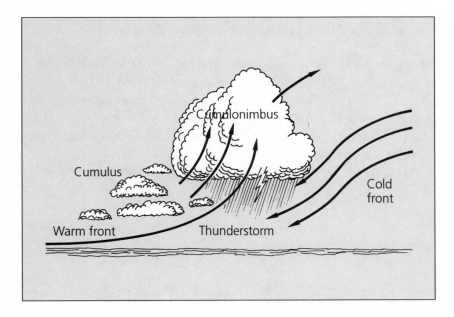

You should head to the closest shore at the first sign of an approaching thunderstorm. Try never to get caught in a thunderstorm. But if this does happen, you should lower the rig onto the water and crouch on the board with your feet close together. This is also the safest position to avoid the unlikely event of being struck by lightning.

CURRENTS AND TIDES

Remember, the deeper the water, the stronger the current or tide. Currents are water movements caused by differences in underwater elevations. Tides are caused by the gravitational pull of the moon and sun. Tides generally occur in coastal waters and do not usually have an effect on lakes. In lakes drained by run-offs or near a hydroelectric dam, some of the most dangerous currents may occur. Generally, these areas are well marked with large warning signs.

When you are just beginning to windsurf, avoid any area that has a strong current or tide.

Pre-Windsurfing Equipment Check

Make it a habit to check your windsurfing equipment thoroughly each time you go out to windsurf. Check all lines very carefully for damage and make sure that they are securely fastened to your equipment. If lines are damaged, replace them immediately with new ones. Also make sure that every part of your rig and windsurfing board is complete and fully functional. If any part shows signs of stress, damage, or is not functional at all, have it repaired or replaced. Also check your windsurfing wetsuit for holes or tears.

It is very difficult and time-consuming if you have to deal with equipment problems in the water. Make a pre-windsurfing check a habit, so that your windsurfing day will be enjoyable.

Transporting Your Windsurfing Board

If you are transporting your windsurfing equipment by car, a roof rack will be necessary. The roof rack should be sturdy and must be able to support a least one hundred fifty pounds. You will also need a set of quick release straps to fasten your board and boom to the roof rack.

It is a good idea to use foam pads on the rack to protect your board, which can be purchased at your local windsurfing shop. Your board should be positioned so that the top surface is facing down and the bow of the board is pointing toward the front of the car. Mast attachments are also available for the roof rack. Always check your roof rack and make sure everything on it is secure before driving to the windsurfing area.

Remember the Following

- Make sure you check on the weather and wind conditions in your windsurfing area before going out.
- Light to gentle breezes that are onshore or parallel to shore are safer.
- Always dress properly for the given climate.

- Get information about your windsurfing spot and find out if there are any dangers.
- Choose only good days to go out windsurfing.
- Make sure you check your equipment before going out.
- Go windsurfing with others. You will be safer, learn faster, and have more fun.
- Respect other water participants and the environment.
- Avoid windsurfing in swimming areas and waters with heavy commercial traffic.
- If you get tired, return to shore and take a break.
- Know the local boating rules, regulations, and the right-of-way rules.
- If you run into problems, stay on your board and try to reach the nearest shore either by luffing your rig, self-rescue, or summoning assistance using a distress signal.

Glossary

Apparent Wind A combination of the true wind and the created wind induced by the movement of the board. This is the wind you feel when you are windsurfing.

Beam Reach The point of sailing 90 degrees to the wind.

Bear Off Turning away from the wind.

Beaufort Wind Scale A method for classifying wind strength, developed by Sir Francis Beaufort.

Broad Reach The fastest point of windsurfing. The course between beam reach and run.

Center of Effort (CE) The point on the sail representing the sum of all the forces acting upon it.

Center of Lateral Resistance (CLR) A point representing the sum of all the forces of resistance offered by all the parts of the board.

Close-Hauled Sailing close to the wind.

Created Wind Wind generated through movement by a person or object.

Current The horizontal movement of water.

Derigging Taking apart the rig for storage or self-rescue.

Eye of the Wind The exact direction from which the wind is coming.

Flotation Aid Lightweight jacket that gives you added buoyancy.

Head Up Turning the board toward the direction of the wind.

Hypothermia A dangerous medical condition brought on by overexposure to cold.

Jibe A turn where the stern of the board passes through the eye of the wind.

Leeward The downwind side of an object.

Lift   The force created when air passes over a sail.

Line   Piece of rope used on a windsurfing board, i.e., downhaul, outhaul, uphaul line.

Luffing   Allowing the sail to flutter with the wind like a flag.

Neoprene   Rubber material used to make wetsuits.

Offshore Wind   A wind blowing away from the shore, which should be avoided by novice windsurfers.

Onshore Wind   Wind blowing toward the shore.

Personal Flotation Device (PFD)   A buoyant vest for windsurfing and boating.

Points of Sail   Words used to describe the angle between the board's course and the wind.

Port   The left-hand side of the board when looking at the bow.

Rigging   Assembling the mast foot, mast, boom, and sail to set up the rig.

Rules of the Road   Rules of right-of-way for different situations. Established to prevent collisions on the water.

Run   Windsurfing directly downwind.

Sea Breeze   Summertime wind on the ocean or large lakes. Sea breeze blows toward the land.

Sheeting In/Out   Adjusting the rig position for more or less power.

Starboard   The right side of the board when looking at the bow.

Steamer   A thick wetsuit with insulating characteristics used in winter or where water is especially cold.

Tacking   A turn where the bow of the board passes through the eye of the wind.

Tide   Caused by the gravitational pull of the moon and sun, which creates the vertical fall and rise of a mass of water.

True Wind   The wind that is blowing when you are standing still.

Wetsuit   A suit that traps water between the suit and your body and keeps you warm while windsurfing.

Windward   The side closest to the wind.

Index

Page numbers in **boldface** refer to illustrations.

WINDSURFING INSTRUCTORS OF
AMERICA (WIA)

For information on windsurfing instruction courses, contact the WIA at P.O. Box 472, 113 Russell Avenue, Stevenson, WA 98648; telephone (509) 427-7111; fax (509) 427-7144.